For Kayden-Marie

"Fannie Lou Hamer's story needs to be told and I can think of no one better than K. A. Ellis to tell it. In this beautiful biography, we see how the gospel compelled this remarkable woman to share the good news of Jesus, pray for her enemies, and combat the injustice around her. May her story inspire us to do the same!"

COURTNEY DOCTOR, Author; Bible Teacher; Director of Women's Initiatives, The Gospel Coalition

"You never know what's in a person till they are bumped and you see what spills out. Fannie Lou got bumped hard and often. What spilled out was a song of praise for God, courage to expose injustice and rescue the weak, practical help for her neighbors, and grace for even people who hurt her. Let's follow Fannie Lou. "

JOHN ENSOR, President of PassionLife

"I LOVE, LOVE, LOVE this book! I have spoken about Fannie Lou Hamer in speeches, written about her, and admired her for years. The fact that another generation will have the opportunity to learn about this great woman makes my heart happy!"

KAY JAMES, Secretary of the Commonwealth of Virginia; President of the Heritage Foundation (2017-2021)

"As a father of three, I know it's important to provide children with clear examples of how Christian convictions drive believers toward redemptive work. K.A. Ellis beautifully illustrates how a deep faith in Christ inspired Hamer's vision, courage, and perseverance."

JUSTIN E. GIBONEY, AND Campaign; Author, *Compassion (&) Conviction*

thegoodbook for children

Fannie Lou Hamer
© K.A. Ellis 2024

Illustrated by Shin Maeng | Design and Art Direction by André Parker
Series Concept by Laura Caputo-Wickham
Published in association with the literary agency of THE GATES GROUP.
"The Good Book For Children" is an imprint of The Good Book Company Ltd.
thegoodbook.com | thegoodbook.co.uk | thegoodbook.com.au
thegoodbook.co.nz | thegoodbook.co.in
ISBN: 9781784989439 | JOB-007593 | Printed in India

Do Great Things for God

Fannie Lou Hamer

The Courageous Woman Who Marched for Dignity

K.A. Ellis

Illustrated by Shin Maeng

Fannie Lou Hamer and her husband, "Pap," were poor, and life was hard. But they looked forward to Sundays, when they gathered at church with God's people in their tiny town in the Mississippi Delta.

Music and preaching, ushers and tambourines —
oh, how they lived when Sunday came!

Inside their church, Mother Hamer sang with the little ones in Sunday school...

This little light of mine, I'm gonna let it shine!
This little light of mine, I'm gonna let it shine!
This little light of mine, I'm gonna let it shine!
Let it shine, let it shine, let it shine!

The children loved to sing with her.

So Mother Hamer sang on.

Fannie had stopped going to school for most of the year when she was six. Her family needed her to help them work in the cotton fields so that they could eat and keep their home.

Because of the color of her skin, Mother Hamer couldn't ride in the front of the buses, go to doctors or hospitals, eat in restaurants, shop in stores, or even vote*. There were laws that stopped her doing all these things.

But Mother Hamer had a dream.

* To vote means to have a say in choosing who will be in charge of your country or area.

There was one way for Fannie and her friends to make their voices heard. They needed to be allowed to vote!

So they marched for the right to vote in many cities. They became known as "the Freedom Fighters." They marched hundreds of miles to show how much they wanted to vote and that they too were true citizens!

The marchers often sang songs from church as they marched.

Oh, freedom over me!
And before I'll be a slave, I'll be buried in my grave
And go home to my Lord and be free!

But the louder they sang, the angrier some people grew.

Even though they hadn't done anything wrong,
Mother Hamer and her friends were arrested
and beaten by policemen, who were
supposed to protect them.

Things were very, very hard for Mother Hamer.

They bombed her house, and she stood.

They threw her in jail, and she sang.

They beat her body, and she prayed.

Fannie prayed for God to have mercy
on the people who hated her so much,
and that kept hate out of her heart.

And because she and her friends were
brave and endured, others grew brave.
More people signed up to vote, and
together they sang and marched even more.

So Mother Hamer prayed on.

Mother Hamer traveled by bus to Washington, D.C.
She wanted the country's biggest decision-makers to
hear about all the horrible things she and her friends
had endured just to make their lives better.

She told those important people to change the rules so
that all people would be heard and all people would be
treated with respect — people of all colors, people who
were rich and people who were poor.

Her voice again carried the fire with which she had told anyone who would listen, all over the country, "Until I'm free, you're not free either!"

She wanted the powerful people in Washington to realize that, as she had proclaimed many times before, "Righteousness exalts a nation, but sin is a reproach to any people" (Proverbs 14:34).

The words of the Bible went straight to their hearts, and they understood; God is most pleased when presidents and leaders do what God says is right!

When the powerful men in Washington changed the rules to let Mother Hamer and her friends vote, they knew they had been seen and heard.

So Mother Hamer kept on.

Mother Hamer thought about new ways to bring life to poor people.

Some of the freedom marchers became freedom farmers.

Together they planted all kinds of crops, and they raised pigs and boars. As they planted more and more, the farm grew, and they fed as many hungry families as they could. They worked hard in the Mississippi heat to sow seeds of hope for a better future.

So Mother Hamer worked on.

Mother Hamer loved babies... But the people who hated her had hurt her so badly that she was unable to have babies of her own.

She and Pap prayed, and guess what God did?

God gave her and Pap four beautiful children to adopt and love as their own.

She was determined that they — and all little children — would have better lives than she did.

She proclaimed to the newspapers the truth that God had buried deep in her heart... that every baby deserves the chance to be born and be loved.

Each life is precious to God, and so each life was precious to Mother Hamer.

Just as she always had, when she was singing in church, when she was working the fields, when she was marching, when she was arrested, when she was making speeches, and when she was standing up for little children...

... Mother Fannie Lou Hamer loved on.

Fannie Lou Hamer

1917 – 1977

"Righteousness exalts a nation,

but sin is a reproach to any people."

Proverbs 14:34

Questions to Think About

1. Which part of Mother Hamer's story did you like best?

2. Mother Hamer prayed and sang and marched because she wanted everyone to be allowed to vote. Can you think of something important to pray about? How will you remember to pray every day?

3. Some of the freedom marchers became freedom farmers, who fed as many hungry families as they could. Do you know of anyone who doesn't have enough food, either in your area or further away? How could you help them?

4. What ideas does Mother Hamer's story give you about how you might serve Jesus when you are older?

5. What is one truth about God that you'd like to remember from this story?

Fannie Lou Hamer

1917 Fannie was born in Montgomery County, Mississippi. She was the youngest of 20 children.

1923 When she was six, Fannie went to work. She picked cotton with her family on a plantation owned by W.D. Marlow. In the winter, when there was less work, she went to school. Fannie loved school, especially reading.

1929 At 12 years old, Fannie had to leave school. Her parents were too old and sick to work, so she needed to work full time to help support her family.

1945 Fannie married Perry Hamer, who was known as "Pap." He drove tractors on the plantation where Fannie labored.

1962 When Fannie tried to vote, she kept being told that she was not allowed to, for different reasons. The state of Mississippi had passed several laws that made it very difficult for Black people to vote in elections. Because Fannie kept trying to vote, she lost her job — but eventually, after she fought hard for her rights, she and others like her were allowed to vote.

1963 Fannie worked for the SNCC (Southern Christian Leadership Conferences), trying to help other Black people be allowed to vote. Once, while she was on her way home, she and her friends were arrested. They were taken to a cell by some policemen, who beat her up so badly that she was left with permanent damage to her body, including to an eye and one of her kidneys.

1964 Fannie helped set up the Mississippi Freedom Democratic Party to try to make sure that Black people in the US could have the same rights as everyone else. She made a speech that was shown on television. She asked if America was really free when she and her friends were being threatened every day.

1965 President Lyndon Johnson signed a law called the "Voting Rights Act." This law made illegal the ways that some people had used to prevent Black men and women, like Fannie, voting.

1969 Fannie gave a speech at the White House in Washington, D.C. She asked people to remember that all lives are precious, included the lives of babies who are still growing in the womb. The same year, Fannie set up the "pig bank." A family could borrow and look after a pig until it had piglets, and then give the pig back and keep the piglets, so that they could become farmers. Later, she bought a large area of land and let people live there and farm the land. It was called the "Freedom Farm."

1977 Fannie Lou Hamer died. She was buried in Ruleville, Mississippi. More than 1,500 people came to her funeral, including the US Ambassador to the United Nations.

NORTH
AMERICA

USA

EU

SOUTH
AMERICA

World Map

Where in the world
did Fannie's story
take place?

ASIA

AUSTRALIA

Interact with Fannie's Story!

All About
Fannie Lou Hamer

4-7s

By: _____

My Drawing of Fannie

When was Fannie born?

_____

Where did Fannie grow up?

_____

What did Fannie fight for her people to be allowed to do?

_____

What Did Fannie Do When...

Circle the Answer

She traveled by bus to Washington, D.C.
Demanded the right to vote OR Went back to school

Her people needed a way to feed their families
Bought everyone food OR Started farms for Black men and women

She was unable to have babies
Became a teacher OR Adopted four children

She determined that all babies deserved to be born
Wrote to the newspapers OR Wrote to local doctors

1

What Are 8 Things You Liked about Fannie's Story?

1.
2.
3.
4.
5.
6.
7.
8.

A
B
C

Remember this Verse Fannie Loved

"Righteousness exalts a nation, but sin is a reproach to any people."

Proverbs 14 v 34

Can you say it all by yourself? ■

Family Activity: Fannie loved worshiping God through hymns. Look up some of the songs she sang and pick one to listen to as you read (or sing!) the lyrics together. What do you like about the song? Draw a picture inspired by the lyrics.

2

FREEDOM FIGHTERS

VOTE

8-11s

Biography Report for
Fannie Lou Hamer

By: _____

My favorite thing about Fannie:
_____
_____

Person from the Bible Fannie reminds me of:
_____
_____

A question I would ask Fannie:
_____
_____

Three words I would use to describe Fannie:
1. _____
2. _____
3. _____

Remember this Verse Fannie Loved

" _____ exalts a _____
but _____ is a
to any _____ "

Proverbs 14 v 34

Can you say it 5 times without looking? ▢

· PASSPORT ·

Fannie Lou Hamer

Year of Birth: _____

Hometown: _____

Job Title: _____

[Draw a Portrait]

Search Online to Find:
Ask an adult about doing this together!

What is the Voting Rights Act of 1965? How did Fannie play a role in its development?
_____
_____

Name 3 things Fannie's "Freedom Farms" allowed black men and women to do for their families.
_____
_____

Who were 3 key figures of the Civil Rights Movement?
_____
_____

1

Tell Fannie's story in your own words. You can even pretend you are Fannie and say "I", thinking about how she might feel.

_____

Can you put these events in order? Number the boxes from 1 to 6.

▢ Fannie started a "Freedom Farm"

▢ Fannie stood up for unborn babies in a speech at the White House

▢ Fannie was told she could not vote

▢ Fannie married Perry "Pap" Hamer

▢ Fannie and her friends were arrested

▢ Fannie helped set up the Mississippi Freedom Democratic Party

Family Activity: Fannie loved worshipping God through hymns. Look up some of the songs she sang and pick one to listen to as you read (or sing!) the lyrics together. What do you like about the song? Draw a picture inspired by the lyrics.

2

Download Free Resources at

thegoodbook.com/kids-resources

Do Great Things for God

Inspiring Biographies for Young Children

Corrie ten Boom
The Courageous Woman and the Secret Room
Laura Caputo-Wickham
Illustrated by Isabel Muñoz

Betsey Stockton
The Girl With a Missionary Dream
Laura Caputo-Wickham
Illustrated by Eunji Jung

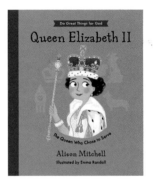

Queen Elizabeth II
The Queen Who Chose to Serve
Alison Mitchell
Illustrated by Emma Randall

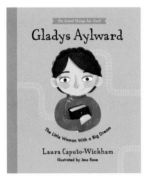

Gladys Aylward
The Little Woman With a Big Dream
Laura Caputo-Wickham
Illustrated by Jess Rose

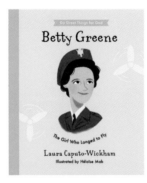

Betty Greene
The Girl Who Longed to Fly
Laura Caputo-Wickham
Illustrated by Héloïse Mab

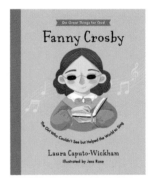

Fanny Crosby
The Girl Who Couldn't See but Helped the World to Sing
Laura Caputo-Wickham
Illustrated by Jess Rose

Maria Fearing
The Girl Who Dreamed of Distant Lands
K. A. Ellis
Illustrated by Isabel Muñoz

Amy Carmichael
The Brown-eyed Girl Who Learned to Pray
Hunter Beless
Illustrated by Héloïse Mab

Helen Roseveare
The Doctor Who Kept Going No Matter What
Laura Caputo-Wickham
Illustrated by Cecilia Messina

thegoodbook.com | thegoodbook.co.uk